# The Plymouth Colony

Gianna Williams and Janet Riehecky

**Gareth Stevens Publishing**
A WORLD ALMANAC EDUCATION GROUP COMPANY

**Please visit our web site at: www.garethstevens.com**
**For a free color catalog describing Gareth Stevens Publishing's list of high-quality**
**books and multimedia programs, call 1-800-542-2595 (USA) or 1-800-387-3178**
**(Canada). Gareth Stevens Publishing's fax: (414) 332-3567.**

**Library of Congress Cataloging-in-Publication Data**

Williams, Gianna Polacco.
    The Plymouth Colony / by Gianna Williams and Janet Riehecky.
      p. cm. — (Events that shaped America)
    Contents: New England's first inhabitants — Plans for a new colony — The journey
and arrival — Settling at Plymouth — Life in Plymouth Colony.
    Includes bibliographical references and index.
    ISBN 0-8368-3224-8 (lib. bdg.)
    1. Massachusetts—History—New Plymouth, 1620-1691—Juvenile literature.
2. Puritans—Massachusetts—History—17th century—Juvenile literature.
3. Pilgrims (New Plymouth Colony)—Juvenile literature. [1. Massachusetts—
History—New Plymouth, 1620-1691. 2. Puritans. 3. Pilgrims (New Plymouth
Colony).] I. Riehecky, Janet, 1953-. II. Title. III. Series.
    F68.W63   2002
    974.4'8202—dc21            2002070756

This North American edition first published in 2002 by
**Gareth Stevens Publishing**
A World Almanac Education Group Company
330 West Olive Street, Suite 100
Milwaukee, WI 53212 USA

This edition © 2002 by Gareth Stevens Publishing.

Produced by Discovery Books
Editor: Sabrina Crewe
Designer and page production: Sabine Beaupré
Photo researcher: Sabrina Crewe
Maps and diagrams: Stefan Chabluk
Gareth Stevens editorial direction: Mark J. Sachner
Gareth Stevens art direction: Tammy Gruenewald
Gareth Stevens production: Susan Ashley

Photo credits: Corbis: pp. 4, 26, 27; Granger Collection: pp. 13, 14, 16, 17; Donald
Hinds: pp. 17, 18, 23, 25; North Wind Picture Archives: cover, pp. 5, 6, 7, 8, 9, 10,
12, 15, 19, 20, 21, 22; Pilgrim Society and Pilgrim Hall Museum: p. 24.

Printed in the United States of America

1 2 3 4 5 6 7 8 9 06 05 04 03 02

# Contents

# Introduction

On September 6, 1620, a ship named the *Mayflower* set sail for North America. On board was a group of **Puritan Separatists**. They were looking for a place to build a community based on their religious beliefs. The journey was difficult and dangerous, and it was the middle of winter before the travelers found a place to settle. In spite of the hardships, the settlers soon founded the **colony** of Plymouth in what is now Massachusetts.

Plimoth Plantation is a living museum where the town of Plymouth has been rebuilt to look like it did in 1627. Everything from people in costume to plants and animals are as authentic as possible.

## Puritans and Separatists

Until 1533, England was a Catholic country. Then King Henry VIII formed the Church of England and made himself its head. Many reforms were made, but some people thought even more were needed.

King James I was head of the Church of England from 1603 to 1625. However, he did not follow the teachings of the Bible exactly, as some Christians thought he should. These Christians wanted to "purify" the church and were known as Puritans. Most Puritans stayed in the Church of England, trying to reform it. Others, known as Separatists, left. They felt their only spiritual leader was God and that they should follow the teachings of the Bible.

The settlers at Plymouth did not call themselves "pilgrims." They were first referred to as pilgrims by William Bradford, governor of Plymouth, in his book *Of Plimoth Plantation 1620–1647*. But the name wasn't generally used to describe the Plymouth colonists until the nineteenth century.

The Separatists who arrived in North America had a strong belief in hard work. This was important for the survival of the colony and later became an important value for many Americans. Unlike other European settlements in North America, the inhabitants of Plymouth worked together as a community. They shared land and food and built houses for each other.

The Plymouth **colonists**, or **Pilgrims**, also had the first written rules of government in North America. They wrote an agreement called the Mayflower **Compact** that said the colony should be governed by "just and equal" laws.

One of the first Plymouth colonists, Priscilla Mullins, steps ashore at Plymouth in 1620.

# New England's First Inhabitants

## Native Americans in New England

In 1600 there were about 120,000 Native Americans living in the area now known as New England. The most powerful group in the area was the Wampanoag. There were several thousand Wampanoag people, belonging to about fifty different tribes. Other peoples in the area included the Massachusets, Narragansetts, and Nausets.

Each Wampanoag tribe was led by a sachem, or chief, and a council of advisors. A grand sachem had authority over all the other chiefs. The Wampanoag and their neighbors did not have written laws but followed long-standing customs.

These lodges were typical New England dwellings in the 1600s. They were built with bark or straw mats laid over wooden poles.

A Wampanoag family is struck down by one of the epidemics that European explorers brought to America.

## Village Life

Individuals did not own land. Instead, groups claimed areas for their villages and farmland as well as for hunting and fishing. Men hunted animals such as deer and rabbits and fished for oysters, salmon, herring, and even turtles. In addition, women grew crops such as corn, beans, and squash and foraged for berries, nuts, and other edible plant foods.

Most Wampanoags lived in lodges or longhouses. These dwellings had rounded roofs and were made of bark or mats woven from reeds or other plants. There were no windows, just a door covered by a mat or animal skin.

## European Contact

The Native people of New England were healthier than Europeans in the early 1600s. Explorers from Europe brought many new diseases, however, such as smallpox. Three **epidemics** between 1614 and 1620 killed many Wampanoags. Because of the epidemics, the Wampanoags were no longer the strongest group in New England.

A few years before the Plymouth colonists came, the site they settled had been home to the Patuxet Wampanoags, but an epidemic had killed them all. That is why the village of Patuxet was empty when the white settlers arrived.

**Savage and Brutish**
"The place . . . [is empty] of all civil inhabitants . . . there are only savage and brutish men which range up and down, little [different] than the wild beasts of the same."

*William Bradford,* Of Plimoth Plantation 1620–1647

# Chapter Two

# Plans for a New Colony

The city of Leiden in the Netherlands (*above*) offered religious freedom to the English Separatists who moved there.

## The Scrooby Separatists

In about 1606, a group of Christians in the English village of Scrooby formed their own Separatist church. This was a crime in England, and they were persecuted. By 1608, 125 Scrooby Separatists had left England for the Netherlands, where they found religious freedom. In 1609, they settled in the city of Leiden. Life was difficult. They could not speak Dutch, and they worked hard for little pay.

As the years passed, the Separatists worried about losing their English traditions and Puritan values. They were also worried because a treaty between the Netherlands and Catholic Spain was about to end. They could then lose their freedom to follow their own religion.

## A New World

Some of the Scrooby Separatists decided to **emigrate** to the English colonies in North America. In 1617, they approached the Virginia Company of London—or London Company—that owned the rights to an area called Virginia in North America. The Separatists asked for a **patent** to settle there.

By February 1620, the Scrooby Separatists had permission to settle in the northern part of Virginia. They bought a small ship, the *Speedwell*, to take them first to England and then to America. Only thirty-five Separatists made the voyage.

On July 22, 1620, the *Speedwell* left the Netherlands for Southampton, England. There it joined up with the *Mayflower*. Its passengers included other English Separatists and a group of non-Puritans. On August 5, 1620, the *Mayflower* and the *Speedwell* set sail from England.

**The Departure from Leiden**

". . . they went aboard and their friends with them, where truly doleful was the sight of that sad and mournful parting, to see what sighs and sobs and prayers did sound amongst them. . . . And then with mutual embraces and many tears they took their leaves one of another, which proved to be the last leave to many of them."

*William Bradford,* Of Plimoth Plantation 1620–1647

Thirty-five Separatists left the Netherlands in July 1620. Because most of the Scrooby Separatists were staying behind, their pastor, John Robinson (*shown center in black*), stayed with them.

# Chapter Three

# The Journey and Arrival

## A Bad Start

The *Mayflower* and the *Speedwell* didn't get far. Twice the travelers had to return to port because the *Speedwell* was leaking. Eventually it was decided that the *Speedwell* would have to be left behind.

The *Mayflower* is tossed around on stormy waves during its journey across the Atlantic Ocean.

As many passengers as possible squeezed aboard the *Mayflower*. When it finally set sail from Plymouth, England, on September 16, 1620, the ship carried about one hundred passengers as well as officers and crew. The passengers included the thirty-five Scrooby Separatists and about sixty-five others, some of them **investors** in the new colony. Myles Standish, a soldier, would be the military commander of the colony. There were also **indentured servants** and craftsmen.

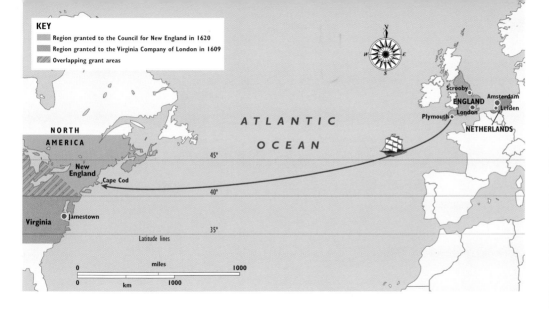

KEY
Region granted to the Council for New England in 1620
Region granted to the Virginia Company of London in 1609
Overlapping grant areas

The *Mayflower* traveled to the east coast of North America and landed in New England. At the time, this was a region that stretched from what is now New Jersey to just north of the Canadian border.

On its journey across the ocean, the *Mayflower* was buffeted by many storms that damaged the ship and forced it off course. Sometimes there was no wind at all and the ship just drifted. During the voyage, a servant named William Butten and one of the sailors died. One woman, Elizabeth Hopkins, gave birth to a boy and named him Oceanus.

## The Wrong Place

On November 9, 1620, after two months at sea, the travelers on the *Mayflower* sighted land. The ship weighed anchor off Cape Cod, Massachusetts, on November 11, 1620. It was north of its destination, which was supposed to be Virginia. Instead, the travelers were in an area called New England. The rights to the area belonged to the Council for New England.

## The *Mayflower*

The *Mayflower* was a small ship compared to those that cross the ocean today. It was probably about 100 feet (30 meters) long and about 25 feet (7 m) wide. Most of the passengers lived and slept in a dark area below deck with no place to wash clothes or take a bath. Along with its many passengers, the *Mayflower* was carrying cargo, including fresh water, food, household items, and animals—such as goats, dogs, and chickens.

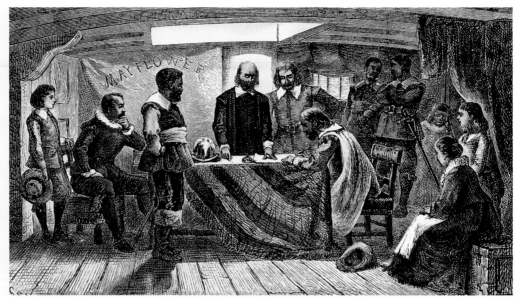

In the cabin of the *Mayflower*, a group of men, including Separatists, non-Separatists, and even servants, sign the Mayflower Compact. No women were allowed to sign it.

## The First Days

The Separatists decided to stay. Because they were not on the London Company's land, they would not be under the company's laws and regulations. The leaders proposed a simple agreement called the Mayflower Compact to govern the new colony. It called for a **civil** government under the rule of the English king. Forty-one men signed the compact, and John Carver was elected as Plymouth's first governor.

**The Mayflower Compact**

"Haveing undertaken . . .to plant ye first colonie in the Northerne parts of Virginia, doe . . . combine ourselves togeather into a civill body politick, for our better ordering, and preservation . . . and by vertue herof to enacte, constitute, and frame such just and equal lawes, **ordinances**, Acts, constitutions, and offices, from time to time, as shall be thought most . . . convenient for ye generall good of ye colonie . . ."

*Part of the Mayflower Compact as recorded by William Bradford,* Of Plimoth Plantation 1620–1647

## Starvation and Disease

While exploration parties looked for a place to settle, many of the people on board the *Mayflower* were getting very sick. Food supplies were low, and the travelers stole food from Native grain stores that they found. Even so, by the middle of December 1620, four people had died.

## Finding Plymouth Harbor

In early December, several men set out in a small boat to find a village site along the coast. During a storm, they noticed what looked like a space between two pieces of land that jutted out. They had found a protected natural harbor.

The men explored the land nearby and discovered a river and cleared fields ready for planting. Large forests could provide firewood and building material. What the settlers had found was the deserted Wampanoag village of Patuxet.

## The *Mayflower* Arrives

The explorers returned to their ship and described the harbor they had found to Captain Jones of the *Mayflower*. The captain located it on his map. King James I had already renamed Patuxet as "New Plymouth" when he had claimed the region for England, and so the settlers named their colony Plymouth. The *Mayflower* set off from Cape Cod, and on December 16, 1620, it was anchored in Plymouth Harbor.

The new settlers finally go ashore at the site chosen for their colony.

# Chapter Four

# Settling at Plymouth

The colonists started building their settlement in deep winter. Their first task was to construct a large house for general use and storage.

## A Daily Struggle

At last, the settlers began building their village. They planned to build a house for each family. Most of them slept on the *Mayflower* and came ashore every day to work. Many settlers were seriously ill and dying, however. During January and February 1621 only six or seven of the colonists were healthy. They did everything they could to take care of the others, but by March only twenty-five men, eight women, and twenty children were still alive out of the original one hundred or so passengers.

There were deaths among the sailors of the *Mayflower* as well, but fewer because they were used to hardship and because they had their own food.

## Samoset

During this time, the settlers had had no direct contact with any Native people who lived in the area. In March 1621, however, a man walked out of the woods and greeted the settlers. His name was Samoset—a sachem from the Abenaki people of what is now Maine—and he was in the area on a hunting trip. Samoset had learned to speak English from sailors who fished along the coast. He told the starving settlers to expect a visit from Chief Massasoit, the grand sachem of the Wampanoag who lived 40 miles (64 kilometers) away in a village on Narragansett Bay.

### A Visit from Samoset

"... there presented himself a savage, which caused an alarm. ... He was a tall straight man, the hair of his head black, long behind, only short before, none on his face at all; he asked some beer, but we gave him strong water and biscuit, and butter, and cheese, and pudding, and a piece of mallard. ... He told us the place where we now live is called Patuxet, and that about four years ago all the inhabitants died of an extaordinary plague."

*Edward Winslow and William Bradford,* Mourt's Relation, *published in 1622*

Samoset arrives at the Plymouth colony in the spring of 1621. It was the first time that the colonists had met a Native American.

When Massasoit arrived to visit the settlers, he brought with him sixty warriors as a show of his power.

## The Arrival of Massasoit

Four or five days later, Chief Massasoit arrived. Massasoit had good reason to hate Europeans because of the way they had treated his people. Massasoit decided to try and keep peace with the colonists, however. The Wampanoags were no longer strong, and perhaps he thought it would be good to have these new settlers as an ally. The Wampanoag and the colonists made an agreement not to harm each other and to defend one another if either group was attacked.

### William Bradford (1590–1657)

William Bradford was a devout Puritan. At the age of twelve, he began attending the Separatist church at Scrooby. When the Separatists left for the Netherlands in 1608, Bradford went with them and became a church leader at eighteen. He was elected Plymouth's governor thirty-one times. He wrote *Of Plimoth Plantation 1620–1647*, an important source of information about the settling of Plymouth.

## Squanto and Survival

Massasoit had brought with him a Patuxet man named Squanto. Squanto was the only known survivor of Patuxet. He had been kidnapped from his village and was in England when the epidemic struck his village. Squanto stayed in Plymouth and taught the colonists many survival skills, including how to **fertilize** their cornfields with fish.

As the weather grew warmer, the colonists grew healthier. Squanto helped them plant corn, barley, and peas. They started vegetable gardens and built better houses.

After Squanto, another Wampanoag man, Hobomok, came to live at Plymouth. Both Squanto and Hobomok were very helpful, and Hobomok stayed for many years.

*Above*: Squanto demonstrates Wampanoag farming methods to the Plymouth colonists.

## Bradford Becomes Governor

The *Mayflower* had stayed through the winter, but on April 5, 1621, it set sail for England, leaving the colonists behind. On June 1, 1621, the Council for New England issued a grant to Plymouth Colony. The colonists now had permission to stay where they were. That summer, Governor Carver died of sunstroke and William Bradford was elected governor. He continued to build a good relationship with the Wampanoag and sent men to defend Massasoit whenever he needed help.

*Below*: Hobomok's reconstructed longhouse at Plimoth Plantation.

A garden was planted at the side of each house in Plymouth as soon as it was built. The gardens contained vegetables, herbs, and medicinal plants.

## A Harvest Celebration

The harvest of 1621 was not large, but the settlers knew they would not starve that winter. The colonists and the Wampanoag held a harvest celebration some time between late September and early November. Massasoit brought ninety warriors with him, greatly outnumbering the fifty or so colonists in Plymouth.

Massasoit sent his men to hunt for deer, and the Wampanoag provided other food as well. The colonists probably served wildfowl, fish, stewed pumpkin, and cooked cornmeal. The visit from the Wampanoag lasted three days.

The winter of 1621 was much less severe than that of 1620, with less illness and fewer deaths. But there were other problems. New settlers arrived, and so there were more mouths to feed. Also, the London investors wanted to be paid for their help. The colonists loaded a ship with furs and timber, but the cargo was stolen by French pirates during the ship's journey to England.

# The Thanksgiving Holiday

The present Thanksgiving Day originates from a Puritan tradition of gathering to thank God when things went well, at any time of the year. The Puritan thanksgiving became an annual event in New England in the eighteenth century. The first national thanksgiving holiday took place in 1777, and it became an annual holiday in 1863. The day it was held varied from year to year. Later in the nineteenth century, Thanksgiving Day began to be connected to the Plymouth colonists. The connection became stronger as time went by. It wasn't until 1941, however, that the fourth Thursday of November was finally set as Thanksgiving Day.

The harvest feast in 1621 was an important show of friendship between the Wampanoag and the Plymouth settlers.

# Chapter Five

# Life in Plymouth Colony

This is the first seal, or official stamp, of Plymouth, issued after the colony acquired its legal status in 1621.

## Governing Themselves

As the colony established itself, the colonists formed their own rules of government. The men who made the rules were Separatists. Even though they weren't the biggest group in the colony, they were the most powerful. This was because only **freemen** could decide laws, and freemen had to be members of the Separatist church. They elected the governor and sat in the General Court that made laws. The laws were strict, and lawbreakers were severely punished.

## Religious Freedom

Although the Separatists had come in search of religious freedom, they did not show it where other religions were concerned. People of other religions were excluded from government in Plymouth, and Native American religions were totally unacceptable.

True religious freedom appeared in New England later, in the Rhode Island colony founded in 1636 by Roger Williams. Williams believed that people should worship—or not—as they chose and that the church should not be involved in government. This was very unusual in the early days of colonial New England. So was Williams' belief that the land belonged to the Native people of New England and not to the English king.

## Plymouth Village

The original town of Plymouth was built on the side of a hill, with a wide street running east to west through its center. By the fall of 1621, the colonists had probably built seven houses and four buildings for storehouses and general use. Each family had its own fenced garden plot.

In 1622, the whole of the town was enclosed with a **palisade**. That June, the settlers heard that Indians had attacked the settlement in Jamestown, Virginia, so they started building a fort on top of the hill. The fort was also where the community worshiped. By 1624, there were about 180 people and 32 houses in Plymouth.

## Owning the Land

After 1623, the Plymouth government allowed the colonists each to farm their own land instead of farming the land as a group. In 1627, the colony's leaders bought the London investors' share of Plymouth. This meant that the colonists no longer owed money to people back in England. The houses, land, and livestock were divided between about fifty-five freemen. The group who bought the investors' share of Plymouth hoped to make money from the colony's fur trade.

An artist's impression of how Plymouth looked in 1622, with the fort at the top of the hill on the right. The palisade built that year is not shown.

For a time, the original fort was also used as a church and meeting house. Attending church services was important in Plymouth's everyday life.

## Everyday Survival

Daily life in early Plymouth was taken up with activities necessary for survival. People had to work hard just to feed themselves, although Sunday was sacred as a day of rest and worship, and no one worked or played that day.

Raising crops was the most important activity. Everyone —men, women, and children—worked in the fields. The cornfields were fertilized with herring caught from the river with a clever system of sliding doors that trapped the fish in a pond as they swam upstream but let the water run through.

## A Child's Life

Children in Plymouth worked much harder than children do today. They labored in the fields, fetched water, dug for **groundnuts**, and tended animals. Children were taught at home and at church. Every day except Sunday was a work day and Sundays were for worship. When they could, children played marbles or ball games and running games.

The men hunted, cleared land, chopped wood, and took turns on guard duty at night. The women cooked, sewed, made household goods, and took care of children and sick people. Most families had servants. Although they took orders and were sometimes poorly treated, servants worked with family members rather than doing all their work for them.

## Plentiful Food

Food was good and plentiful in Plymouth Colony. The Wampanoag taught colonists which wild plants were edible. The woods held many kinds of wildfowl, and there was lots of seafood. Like the Wampanoags, the colonists preserved fish and game by drying and smoking it so that it could be stored for times when food was scarce. Later, when cattle were brought to Plymouth, the settlers had milk and beef.

**Wholesome and Healthful**

"The wholesomeness of the place, and its healthfulness is accompanied by so much plenty of fish and fowl everie day in the year, that I know of no place that can match it."

*John Pory, a visitor to the Plymouth Colony in 1622*

This interior of a house at Plimoth Plantation is typical of the early days. The houses had one main room with a fireplace and a small upstairs loft. There were few windows, and the floors were made of packed earth.

Soap making was one of the women's many tasks. First they made lye, a good cleaning agent, by pouring water over ashes. The water dripped through, drawing with it a substance called potash. The potash was boiled to turn it into lye. Then the lye was mixed with animal fats to make soap.

## Making Everything

Nearly everything in the colony had to be made by hand. From soap and candles to barrels and farm tools, the colonists had to make what they had not brought with them.

People did not have money, and so they paid each other by exchanging their labor. For instance, a load of firewood could be exchanged for a pair of shoe soles.

## Industry and Commerce

In 1622, the Plymouth colonists began to trade tools, weapons, and trinkets—such as chains, mirrors, and glass beads—with the Wampanoag for grain and meat. Soon, they were also trading for furs and other items that could be sent to England. Fur, especially

Samplers were sewn by girls and women. This one was made by Loara, daughter of Plymouth's military commmander Myles Standish. It was made in 1653 and is America's earliest known sampler.

beaver, was very popular in Europe. By 1625, the colonists were buying furs from Native groups in present-day Maine. A few years later, Plymouth colonists began to sell cattle and grain to other settlers in New England and even farther south.

## Plymouth Colony Grows

In 1630, Plymouth received a new patent that granted them land on the Kennebec River, now in Maine, where the colony had a fur-trading post. The patent also granted Cape Cod to the colony.

By the early 1630s, people started to form new settlements, the first being the town of Duxbury across Plymouth Bay. Soon, there were several other communities, such as Scituate, Barnstable, and Yarmouth. By 1640, Plymouth Colony had expanded to eight towns and 2,500 people.

These hides are drying in Hobomok's longhouse at Plimoth Plantation. Native people dried the hides before selling them to white traders. The furs were then packed in barrels and sent to England.

# Conclusion

A ship called *Mayflower II* has been built the same way the first *Mayflower* would have been.

## Colonial New England

From 1630, other colonies were founded in New England. The biggest was Massachusetts Bay Colony, which brought 20,000 settlers to the region between 1630 and 1643. As white settlement grew, the Native people of New England lost all their tribal lands.

On October 17, 1691, Plymouth was declared part of its neighbor Massachusetts. Massachusetts remained a British colony until the colonies declared their independence in 1776.

## Plymouth Today

Every year, about a million people visit Plymouth's historical sites, such as Burial Hill, the site of one of the first forts built by the Pilgrims. Plymouth boasts more than a dozen museums, including a Pilgrim wax museum and a children's museum.

Plimoth Plantation is a living history museum that has a reconstruction of the village as it was in 1627.

It is unlikely that the *Mayflower* passengers chose Plymouth Rock as a convenient spot to land, but a myth about the rock has existed since 1741. Many vistors go to see the rock in Plymouth Harbor.

The village contains houses, the first fort, pens for livestock, gardens, and fields for crops, all of which are kept and worked just as the colonists would have done. Hobomok's homesite nearby is a replica of a Wampanoag dwelling where visitors can see demonstrations of Native skills and crafts.

## The *Mayflower II*

The *Mayflower II* is about 3 miles (5 km) away, near Plymouth Rock in the harbor. It is a full-scale reproduction of a seventeenth-century merchant ship of the same type as the *Mayflower*. Visitors to the ship can learn the story of the original voyage and the settlers' first winter, when most of them lived on the *Mayflower*.

### Founding Fathers

The Plymouth settlers are sometimes known as the "Founding Fathers." This is because the first English settlements in North America are considered by some people to be the foundation of the United States of America.

# Time Line

| | |
|---|---|
| 1606 | Scrooby Separatists found their own church. |
| 1609 | Scrooby Separatists settle in Leiden, Netherlands. |
| 1617 | Epidemic kills inhabitants of Patuxet village. |
| 1620 | February: Scrooby Separatists receive a patent to settle in Virginia. |
| | July 22: Thirty-five Separatists leave Leiden for England. |
| | August 5: *Mayflower* and *Speedwell* make first attempt to leave for North America. |
| | September 16: *Mayflower* sets sail alone for North America. |
| | November 11: *Mayflower* anchors in present-day Provincetown Harbor and Mayflower Compact is drawn up. |
| | December 10: Explorers find Plymouth Harbor. |
| | December 16: *Mayflowe*r anchors at Plymouth Harbor. |
| 1621 | March 16: Samoset visits Plymouth Colony. |
| | March: Massasoit visits Plymouth Colony, bringing Squanto. |
| | April: *Mayflower* returns to England. |
| | Summer: John Carver dies and William Bradford becomes governor. |
| | Fall: Wampanoag and Plymouth settlers hold three-day harvest feast. |
| | November: More settlers arrive from England. |
| 1622 | November: Squanto dies. |
| 1623 | April: Colonists switch from communal farming to individual plots. |
| 1627 | Colonists buy out London investors. |
| 1630 | New patent sets Plymouth boundaries. |
| | Massachusetts Bay Colony is founded. |
| 1636 | Roger Williams founds Rhode Island Colony. |
| 1691 | October 17: Plymouth becomes part of Massachusetts. |

# Things to Think About and Do

## On the *Mayflower*

Read Chapter Three about the colonists' journey to and arrival in America. Imagine you are a passenger on the *Mayflower*, on your way to North America with your family. Write three diary entries: one for the day you leave England, one for a day in the middle of the journey, and one for the day you arrive at Plymouth Harbor. Describe your feelings—are you excited, scared, or bored? Give your impressions of the ship, the passengers, and your arrival.

## A Compact for Today

Look at the quotation from the Mayflower Compact that is on page 12. The men on the *Mayflower* decided they would form their own government and make laws that would be for the general good of the colony. Imagine you were starting a new colony today, and write your own compact. How would your government be chosen? Would you allow your community to be run by church leaders? What would your laws be?

## Different Ways of Thinking and Believing

Look at the quotes on pages 6 and 7. Both were written by early settlers in New England. What do the quotes tell you about the people who wrote them and their attitudes toward Native people? You can read about William Bradford on page 16 and about Roger Williams on page 20. In what way was Roger Williams so different from other Puritans, including Separatist Puritans, who came to New England in the early 1600s?

# Glossary

| | |
|---|---|
| **civil:** | to do with citizens and ordinary people, rather than religious or military authorities. |
| **colonist:** | person who lives in a colony. |
| **colony:** | settlement, area, or country owned or controlled by another nation. |
| **compact:** | agreement. |
| **emigrate:** | leave home to go and live somewhere else. |
| **epidemic:** | something, especially a disease, that spreads quickly and affects lots of people. |
| **fertilize:** | add substances to soil to make it better for growing plants. |
| **fowling:** | hunting and killing wildfowl. |
| **freeman:** | originally one of the forty-one signers of the Mayflower Compact. The number of freemen slowly increased in Plymouth, however, as other reliable men applied to be and were accepted as freemen. |
| **groundnut:** | plant with an edible root. |
| **indentured servant:** | worker who agrees to work for a set period of time in exchange for an opportunity offered by an employer. |
| **investor:** | person who gives money for a project, hoping that it will be successful and that he or she will make a profit. |
| **ordinance:** | local rule or law. |
| **palisade:** | wooden fence made of large, pointed stakes. |
| **patent:** | exclusive right to use or earn money from something. |
| **pilgrim:** | person who goes on a religious journey; also used to mean a Plymouth colonist or other early white settler in North America. |
| **Puritan:** | Christian who wanted to purify the Church of England. |
| **Separatist:** | Christian who separated from the Church of England. |

# Further Information

## Books

Bruchac, Joseph. *Squanto's Journey*. Silver Whistle, 2000.

Erdosh, George. *Food and Recipes of the Pilgrims (Cooking Throughout American History)*. Powerkids Press, 1998.

Grace, Catherine O'Neill. *1621: A New Look at Thanksgiving*. National Geographic Society, 2001.

McGovern, Ann. *If You Sailed on the Mayflower in 1620*. Scholastic, 1993.

Sita, Lisa. *Indians of the Northeast: Traditions, History, Legends, and Life*. Gareth Stevens, 2001.

Waters, Kate. *Tapenum's Day: A Wampanoag Indian Boy in Pilgrim Times*. Scholastic, 1996.

## Web Sites

**www.pilgrimhall.org** Pilgrim Hall Museum has the largest collection of Plymouth artifacts, many of them shown here with interesting details.

**www.plimoth.org** Plimoth Plantation web site offers pictures of the reconstructed village, plus plenty of good information about the Wampanoag, the first settlers, and the daily lives of both groups.

**www.bostonkids.org/teachers/TC/** the Children's Museum, Boston, and the Wampanoag people offer a joint web site about Wampanoag culture and history.

## Useful Addresses

**Plimoth Plantation**
P.O. Box 1620
Plymouth, MA 02362
Telephone: (508) 746-1622

# Index